Contents

Bodies come in all kinds of shapes, colours and sizes!

All Kinds of

Bodies

Written by Judith Heneghan

Illustrated by Ayesha Rubio
and Jenny Palmer

FRANKLIN WATTS

LONDON • SYDNEY

First published in Great Britain in 2019
by The Watts Publishing Group
Copyright © The Watts Publishing Group 2019

Designer: Little Red Ant
Editor: Nicola Edwards

HB ISBN: 978 1 4451 6110 5
PB ISBN: 978 1 4451 6111 2

Printed in Dubai

Franklin Watts
An imprint of Hachette Children's Group
Part of The Watts Publishing Group
Carmelite House
50 Victoria Embankment
London EC4Y 0DZ
An Hachette UK Company

www.hachette.co.uk
www.franklinwatts.co.uk

Bodies can be curved, straight, round, smooth, lumpy, muscly, thin, big or little.

They also change as we get older.

There are so many shades for the skin we are covered in.

And every shade or skin type
needs protecting from the sun.

Many of us grow hair on our heads and bodies.

This might be a little,
or a lot.

We can cover it,
cut it, colour it –
or not.

11

People from the same family may share similar features.

We are twins.

But not always!

Families come in different shapes
and sizes, too.

Our bodies help us communicate and show others how we are feeling. Some people speak with their mouths.

Hello!

Others speak with their hands.

Thank you!

Our bodies let us know what we need,
in all kinds of ways.

When I'm hungry, my tummy rumbles.

When I'm hot, my body starts to sweat and I feel thirsty.

When I'm cold, my teeth chatter and my skin feels shivery.

When I'm tired, I yawn and fall asleep.

Most of us feel unwell at some point in our lives.

Our bodies get sick, or sore.

So we visit the doctor.

Some kinds of bodies need
a little extra help.

I have asthma, so sometimes
I get out of breath and feel
extra tired. My inhaler helps
me recover.

I have diabetes, so I take medicine called insulin every day.

My eyes make things look blurry. Glasses help me see better.

Different bodies are good at different things.

And some things that seem hard at first get easier with practice!

Our differences make the world more interesting.

If our bodies were all the same, how would we recognise each other?

No one else has a body quite like mine, or yours.

Every body is unique.

Every body
is amazing.

Notes for teachers, parents and carers

This book is designed to help children feel good about their own bodies and value the wonderful diversity of people they encounter in the world around them. Children take their first cues about themselves and their peers from their parents or primary carers. If you are reading this book with a child in your care, encourage them to point out what they see in the pictures. Give them permission to be curious, to observe similarities and differences, and answer their questions with the following headings in mind.

Be inclusive

Parents, teachers and carers can help children appreciate all kinds of bodies by making sure the books they read and the programmes they watch are as inclusive as possible. Normalise difference. Seek out positive role models for all children and celebrate each person's unique talents, regardless of gender, ethnicity, size, age or disability. Show that the way we look does not define who we are. Point to the achievements of diverse sports stars, scientists, artists or innovators who have challenged other people's preconceptions and prejudices.

Be positive

Children are helped to develop a positive body image when parents, teachers and carers talk about their own bodies in positive ways. We can also encourage children to show us what they can do, and praise them when they try something new.

Challenge stereotypes

Stereotypes are lazy and misleading assumptions, such as 'pink is for girls' or 'boys prefer sport'. Ask children whether they have come across any stereotypes that they think are unfair. This is a good starting point for talking about the harm that stereotypes can do. Encourage open discussion about different kinds of bodies to help children develop empathy and challenge stereotypical assumptions about disability, gender, body shape or ethnicity, for example.

Promote a healthy lifestyle

A healthy lifestyle isn't about looking different on the outside – it's about feeling good on the inside. A combination of a healthy, balanced diet and regular exercise helps children feel well and energised. It also helps them get a good night's sleep. Encourage positive action, such as eating more fruit and vegetables or taking up a fun new sport or hobby.

Your body belongs to you

Children need to learn that their body belongs to them and nobody else. This promotes self-esteem, and also gives them confidence to say no to unwelcome or inappropriate touching. Teachers can help by establishing clear boundaries for everyone in the classroom – no touching in any area covered by underwear, for example. All responsible adults need to be sensitive to signs of abuse that children may disclose in a classroom setting.

Activity – what do you see?

Ask a group of children to describe their own skin colour and hair. Help them identify interesting words to describe colour, shade and texture. When each child has thought about themselves in this way, ask them to describe their neighbour with equal care. Follow this by suggesting they paint portraits of each other. This activity helps children learn about and appreciate the ways we are all different, and the same.

Useful words

asthma   an illness that makes your chest feel tight. People with asthma feel out of breath more easily.

birthmark   a patch of skin that is different in colour or texture to the rest of your skin – something you have had since you were born.

diabetes   an illness caused by too much sugar in your blood.

features   the different parts of your face such as eyes, freckles or wrinkles.

inhaler   a device for giving medicine that helps people with asthma breathe more easily.

sweat   the moisture on our skin when we feel hot.

unique   special, the only one of something.

Index